Day Drinking and Daffodils

Madeline H-Bush

BookLeaf Publishing

India | USA | UK

Presentation by *BookLeaf Publishing*

Web: www.bookleafpub.com

E-mail: info@bookleafpub.com

ISBN: 9789357611992

First edition 2021

DEDICATION

Mum and Dad–

Thank you for always being my biggest support. I love you.

Lucky,

I wish I could have celebrated this with you. I love you.

ACKNOWLEDGEMENT

First and foremost, I want to thank my amazing parents, Silke and Kevin, who support me through all of my creative endeavors. I specifically want to thank my mum for helping me in this journey to bring my work to life and for giving me (sometimes) way too honest feedback for my liking.

I also want to thank my grandparents, Therese and Ray, and Ted and Lorraine. Thank you for always believing in my ability to accomplish my goals and for constantly checking in on me.

To my fur-brothers, Spardy, Percy and Hercules; for always listening and being a warm hug to cry into.

To my Lucky, I wish you were here for this as you have always been my writing buddy. I miss your soft snores as my white noise when writing but, you are always close to my heart.

Thank you to the wonderful team at BookLeaf Publishing for making this collection come to life. You guys have been amazing to work with.

Thank you to Grace, Lachlan, Mikayla, Ashleigh and Ebony for always listening to my thoughts and giving me opinions throughout working on this collection, sometimes at the most random hours of the day. You guys are the best friends I could ever ask for and you guys have supported all my ideas and dreams for as long as you've known me. I love you guys.

Thank you to the rest of my friends and family for believing in me. You know who you are.

PREFACE

Day Drinking and Daffodils is my first collection of prose poetry. These poems were born from heartbreak and emotional toxicity and slowly it became a beautiful but cathartic way of me unloading my innermost feelings. The beginning of the collection is made up of simpler poems written as a teenager, explaining the falsehood of heart break and how as a teenager I thought this type of love was the be all and end all. The middle of the collection is about loss and grief, not in the sense of physical death, but the emotional death of relationships both platonic and romantic. Finally, the last part of the collection is about the acceptance of self love and expressing femininity and growth through age and maturity.

Falling

It started with a hello and a boyish smirk.
I think I fell right there.

4am thoughts

4am became my favourite time of the day. You would stay up and talk to me until our eyes were stinging, craving for sleep. We would look like zombies the next day, deep purple hues lined under our eyes, making them look sunken. We had so many thoughts to share, so many secrets and promises. Now at that time, I sleep. I no longer have a need to stay awake till then, when you have become a stranger. One I would recognise all too well if I saw you again.

You

You were there when I needed you.

Green Eyes

I helped you win her over.
T'was fun in the beginning;
Helping her fall for you I mean.
I just couldn't shake your green eyes
Out of my mind though.

Salt in the Cut

Even in the shower, the
Salt from my tears stings the
Cuts on my tongue from biting too hard.
It's better to stay silent.

Narcissus

Like Narcissus, you too fell in love with yourself.

Like Nemesis, I left you to be lost in the reflection pool of your ego for eternity.

Mama's Boy

Even though you were a 'Mama's Boy',
You sure as hell didn't treat me with the same
respect.

I still wonder how you are the way you are,
When your mum is the loveliest person.

Over

I'm not sure how many times
I had to tell you we were over,
but I think it was six or seven.

seventy-five

There are up to seventy-five different forms of poetry and you haven't even made it into one of mine.

WARNING!

Sleep after crying makes the headache worse.

Eclectic Trauma

Majority of my music is attached to bad
memories and that's on coping mechanisms.

Bread Crumbs

If you didn't know, there's a thing in dating called 'bread crumbing'. It means that just as you are getting over them, they come back to give you a sense of hope and you continue to chase them.

I was the stupid idiot who followed the crumbs for two years.

Day Drinking

There is nothing more embarrassing than getting drunk from day drinking at a party and crying your eyes out in front of thirty people, just because you broke up with someone a week before that.

Maybe it was just the way he moved on so fast?

'Emerald Eyes'

Oh, how I wished this song was about me.

Supermarket
Flowers

You're the kind of flowers that you already buy
dead from a supermarket.

A Dedication

This one goes out to all the kids who had to muffle the noise because they cried so hard. I'm so sorry.

It get's better, I promise.

Remission

I cut the growth that you were from my skin.
I was left all bloody, with pieces missing.

Now, it's scabbed over and I am healing.
You are not coming back.

Control

I don't find comfort in solitude.
Solitude finds comfort in me.

Seeds

Today I planted the seeds,
For a new me to grow.

I watched the water soak into the soil,
and said a little prayer over them.

'God, please let this bunch survive
Through all the elements.

Through day and night,
Through thick and thin

And most of all, let her thrive.'

best friends > boyfriends

Because of you, I learnt that my best friends are my true loves.

They stay, you don't.

Daffodils

One day, when this chapter is all finished,
I will lay in a field of daffodils and be reborn.

I will be reborn as an independent young woman
Who doesn't need a man to dictate her decisions.

I will lay in between the Daffodils and
Soak in the sunshine and blue sky.

I will thread my fingers through the
Grass and feel the dirt under my nails.

I will smell the Daffodils and remember
That I am stronger without you.

Because you are no Daffodil,
You're a Buttercup.